Biedermeier

4

5

Angus

Bieder

Abbeville Press

Wilkie

meier

Publishers, New York

A t the peak of the Napoleonic wars, in 1806, Emperor Franz I issued a decree ordering all objects of gold and silver under public, church, and private ownership to be turned over to the state.[1] Whatever was collected was melted down to alleviate the financial distress of the era. The Napoleonic wars had left the Austrian Empire in a state of bankruptcy. Only a few articles escaped this massive wave of destruction, and they had been paid for dearly in gold and silver coinage. These drastic circumstances slowly abated after peace was declared in 1815. However, as a result of the persistently high intrinsic value of these commodities, the gold and silver industries made only a modest recovery during the Biedermeier era, even though the economy as a whole was quite prosperous by 1820. And owing to the relatively modest means of the bourgeoisie, silver was never a common artifact or utensil in the Biedermeier household.

Perhaps for this reason, no uniform stylistic element is evident in the silver which was made during the period. Parallel developments of several styles, however, were adopted for the manufacture of silver. Highly ornamental silver was produced concurrently in Baroque, Gothic, and French Rococo styles. This resulted in a hybrid style for upper-middle-class citizens, who, without sufficient means, attempted to imitate the aristocracy. The result was a silver that imitated earlier forms but was characterized by inferior workmanship.

Silver

In contrast to these ornamental styles, the most striking (and perhaps indigenous) forms which emerged were the very plain, simple, utilitarian designs for silver. These represented a radical departure from all historical traditions and were boldly innovative. In Vienna, the ornamental style of the Empire also found its way into the culture. Craftsmen modeled their work directly on the earlier French Empire form and, as is evident in the candlesticks in figure 163, the rosette pattern became an adopted motif—one whose tie with nature clearly delighted the Biedermeier generation.

Because of the absence of silver objects (such as candlesticks,

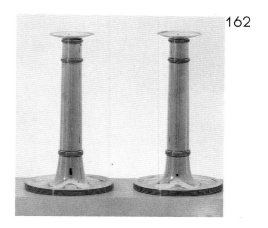

162

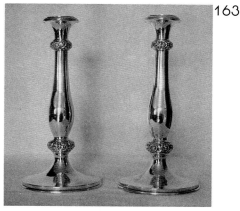

163

Fig. 162
A pair of silver candlesticks, Vienna, 1819. PRIVATE COLLECTION, NEW YORK CITY

Fig. 163
A pair of silver candlesticks with a rosette motif. Maker's mark "Vienna, 1828." PRIVATE COLLECTION, GRAZ

of wooden candlesticks resting on ivory mounts (fig. 164) is a good example of the simple forms favored at the time. Certainly, the contrast of wood and ebonizing, highlighted by the touch of ivory, is reminiscent of Biedermeier furniture.

Chandeliers

Chandeliers were another practical item of the era. Often they were made from carved wood and then gilded. These were delicately handcrafted objects of intricate detail which customarily borrowed motifs from the familiar Neoclassical repertoire.

Biedermeier craftsmen were constantly in search of inexpensive methods by which they could produce objects in quantity. They discovered an alternative to ornamental carving by producing a composition material consisting of paper, sawdust, and glue—or sometimes ground stone pulp and glue—which could be molded and then gilded after it dried. An armature of wood was constructed and then built up with decorative layers of composition material, which was then molded. Both wooden chandeliers and oil-burning lamps were often decorated in this manner.

Glass was still another alternative material for chandeliers. However, glass, like bronze, was not an indigenous substance and was expensive. Hence, it was not used as extensively as wood. Candles and oil-burning lamps continued to be the only sources of artificial illumination inside the home. Gas lighting was not introduced domestically in Europe until the mid-1840s.[2] Therefore, the chandelier and the oil lamp were produced as both utilitarian and decorative items.

Social Artifacts

Homemade gifts and souvenirs were another important art form of the period. These were produced for birthdays, anniversaries, sentimental occasions, and exchanges based on domestic etiquette—all highly valued excuses to make a fuss in this era of treasures and trifles. Fascinations of the period included a passion for beadwork, which was used to decorate ladies' handbags, gloves, and hairpieces, as well as a sentimental affinity for creating jewelry from braided hair. The latter was an intricate process, used for making pins, rings, and medallions—sometimes worn as decorations, and sometimes framed for display and hung on the wall.

The custom of keeping souvenir scrapbooks and diaries was also common. These were often pocket-sized and were carried around from place to place so that friends, relatives, and admirers could write sweet nothings and sketch pretty pictures of memorable times in them.

Fig. 168
A cut-glass chandelier. PRIVATE COLLECTION, LOCUST VALLEY, NEW YORK

Fig. 169
A wood and gilded composition-material chandelier. PRIVATE COLLECTION, NEW YORK CITY

Fig. 170
Detail of the base of a wood and gilded composition-material chandelier. PRIVATE COLLECTION, CHICAGO

As early as the eighteenth century, social visiting was a customary pastime in aristocratic society and bourgeois circles. Etiquette prescribed a rigid, conservative code of manners for all occasions, and so a visitor always carried a personal calling card. These mementos developed from simple visiting cards into much more elaborate, decorative, and expensively created tokens. As an unannounced social visit was considered impolite, it was necessary to leave one's card (or have it delivered by a servant) and then await a reply. The visiting card also served as a token of goodwill, for the nature of polite social visits was concentrated on official occasions, which occurred usually during the holidays.

Glass

Fig. 171
A Viennese Ranftbecher
(beaker) painted by Anton
Kothgasser. PRIVATE COLLECTION,
VIENNA

In the field of decorative arts, the Biedermeier period is remembered, above all, for its exquisite production of porcelain and glass.
At the outset of the nineteenth century the glass industry of Bohemia
was extremely active: forty thousand people were employed at
sixty-six factories to produce glass in all forms and for all purposes.[3]
Glass products served as bottles, beakers, vases, phials, chandeliers,
and drinking glasses, and were also purely decorative objects. This
latter consideration was instrumental in promoting the industry, for
friendship was sentimentalized and all anniversaries carefully ac-
knowledged. A souvenir, token of affection, or commemorative
object was often fashioned from glass. Keepsakes and presents
produced for these occasions boasted a variety of decoration, which
included views of the city, landscapes, portraits, flowers, animals,
emblems, allegories, and fine calligraphy.

The revival of the art of glass-making and glass-engraving was
fueled by middle-class prosperity following the Napoleonic wars.
Clear-cut glass was superseded by vividly colored examples and by
engraved glass. The forms became more massive, and intricately
cut cylindrical shapes were the most common. Samuel Mohn introduced the technique of transparent enamel painting on glass upon
his arrival in Vienna in 1811. Eventually, the greatest Biedermeier
glass engravers and painters worked to the order of private clients.[4]

Three additional types of glass were developed during the period. They remain characteristic examples. Hyalith was a dense,
opaque glass of red or black whose decoration was achieved by
fire gilding, and was possibly inspired by Wedgwood *rosso antico*
and black basalt pottery.[5] Lithyalin was a polished opaque glass
modeled in red and other strong colors, which imitated semipre-
cious stones. It was created by Friedrich Egermann and used in a
wide variety of objects and different styles of decoration between
1828 and 1840.[6] Finally, Annagrün glass had a yellowish-green
fluorescent hue achieved by adding uranium to the color stain. It
was developed by a German, Josef Riedel, circa 1830, who
quaintly named the technique after his wife.[7]

The glass industry flourished in Bohemia throughout the nineteenth century; the Biedermeier era was the zenith for its production
and remains an identifiable period in which more inventions
evolved in the industry than at any other time. Workmanship was
sophisticated and talent among glass painters was particularly fine.

One name which is inextricably linked to hand-painted glass of
the period is that of Anton Kothgasser. He was familiar to the Viennese as a talented porcelain painter. At the same time, he began
painting miniature portraits, landscapes, and genre scenes on glass

to supplement the modest income he earned at Vienna's Royal Imperial Porcelain Factory. Some of the most valuable glass which survives is associated with his hand. The form of glass he produced was known as the "Ranftbecher," a type of low beaker with a tapering, or waisted, body which stood on a thick cogwheel base often decorated with transparent enameling or gilding.[8] Figures 171 and 172 show excellent examples of Kothgasser's expertise at glass painting. Figure 172 depicts a familiar scene of everyday Vienna in front of Saint Stephen's cathedral, a focal point of Viennese religious life. The quintessential scene of horse-drawn carriages in the street and groups of people casually strolling through the square typifies the relaxed bourgeoisie who took pleasure in venturing out of doors for their daily constitutional.

In figure 171, an allegorical scene of nature points to the valued work ethic of the time. The oversized hive with its swarm of bees suggests nature as a parallel of the industrious spirit of bourgeois life. The upright middle-class citizen was happy to own such a symbolic work of art, which aptly reflected the assiduous energy and goals of the Biedermann.

Fig. 172
A Viennese Ranftbecher painted by Anton Kothgasser, depicting the exterior of Saint Stephen's Cathedral. PRIVATE COLLECTION, VIENNA

Fig. 173
A Viennese Ranftbecher, circa 1830, painted by Jacob Schuhfried, an associate of Anton Kothgasser, which is decorated with a representation of the interior of the Seitenstettengasse Synagogue in Vienna. GIFT OF DR. HARRY G. FRIEDMAN, COLLECTION OF THE JEWISH MUSEUM, NEW YORK CITY

172

173

Fig. 174
A hand-painted and parcel-gilt plate with a flower motif. Manufactured by KPM, Berlin, circa 1830. PRIVATE COLLECTION, NEW YORK CITY

Fig. 175
A breakfast service manufactured by KPM, Berlin, circa 1830. COLLECTION OF THE BERLIN MUSEUM

174

175

Porcelain

In contrast to the glass industry, whose production was spread throughout Bohemia, the concentration of the finest porcelain was in Vienna. The Royal Imperial Porcelain Factory, founded in 1718, was run by the state. From 1805 to 1827, under the administration of Matthias Niedermayer, the production of fine china surpassed that of any other period of the nineteenth century.[9] The scope of the Viennese Biedermeier porcelain made at the time stretches from simple sprays of flowers to lavish gold relief and includes intricately painted scenic representations and portraits. Under Niedermayer, a strict division of labor, which was established in the eighteenth century, was continued at the factory. This ensured that specialists in every field of porcelain painting worked solely in their particular forte. "White corps" painters were responsible for the white glazing on the underlying foundation, and the decorative treatment was provided by one of the color specialists in either portrait, landscape, flower, or decorative motifs.[10] The separation of activities provided greater expertise in any given field.

Those painters who specialized in landscape were inspired by local surroundings, and those skilled in portrait and flower painting often copied examples in local art collections. Actual examples in Vienna's botanical gardens and the many dignitaries who visited Vienna supplied further subject matter. As for those who specialized in design, a competition was organized by the factory which awarded bonuses for innovative designs; hence, these painters were constantly challenged to originate new forms.[11]

In Berlin, the KPM porcelain factory supplied society with similarly styled examples of porcelain, and there was also a celebrated factory situated in Meissen.

In form, porcelain of the Biedermeier era was aesthetically pure and classically inspired. Certain examples, such as in figure 174 from Berlin, circa 1830, appear frugally painted with a mere band of gilt encompassing a bouquet of wildflowers. Others display a wide range of color or a painted overglaze, completely covering the piece.

Several factories founded in Bohemia at the end of the eighteenth century were also capable of producing a more economical line of porcelain, fashioned from local clay. Eventually their presence competed significantly with the Viennese establishment, and in 1864 the formerly dominant state porcelain factory was compelled to abandon its production to the private industry, which had gained an insurmountable foothold in Bohemia.[12] However, the finest porcelain was always associated with Viennese production.

Figs. 176, 177
Two hand-painted and parcel-gilt plates from the Viennese Porcelain Factory, circa 1830.
PRIVATE COLLECTION, NEW YORK CITY

Clocks

Like the porcelain and glass industries, the manufacture of clocks was well established prior to the Biedermeier period. Nonetheless, many innovative examples were produced between 1815 and 1830. The successful Viennese and German clock industry looked to French and English prototypes for inspiration, adopting forms of case structure and mechanism. However, the Viennese and German industries also produced outstanding original designs. In Austria, the case structure was often pared down to a minimum, whereas an unparalleled degree of refinement governed the regulating mechanism and the faces of clocks. [13] Artistic mastery balanced fine workmanship.

In timepieces of the era, a distinction was made between clockmakers and watchmakers. Clocks were produced in many forms, including mantelpiece clocks, wall or bracket clocks, table clocks, and grandfather clocks, whereas pocket watches and travel timepieces were made in lesser quantity. Figure 178 shows a min-

Fig. 178
A pocket-watch stand veneered in mahogany and contrasting fruitwoods with bronze and ivory mounts. Probably Austrian. PRIVATE COLLECTION, WEST GERMANY

Fig. 179
A mahogany, birch, and bird's-eye maple clock. Signed "Michael Zanzig, Munich." PRIVATE COLLECTION, WEST GERMANY

179

iature Neoclassical temple which was designed to house one's pocket watch. Customarily, it would be placed on a night table or in an appropriate spot in a bedroom where it would be easily visible. The notion of a Neoclassical monument made for a watch is delightfully appropriate to the period.

Figure 179, an example of a southern German clock, circa 1800, is signed by Michael Zanzig, a clockmaker from Munich. The shape of the curvaceous side stretchers is a precursor of Biedermeier form, but the applied surface mounts and alabaster finial maintain an Empire feeling. In contrast, the shape of a later German example, circa 1820 (fig. 181), is more typical of pure Biedermeier design. The contrasting cherry and ebonized woods are immediately reminiscent of the warm tones of the contemporary furniture. Its pleasing, supple line is characteristic of the finest clocks made during the Biedermeier era, and, at the same time, the clock is surprisingly similar to the style of Art Nouveau, which was not to appear for some eighty years.

Finally, the exquisite Berlin grandfather clock in figure 180 is a rare and unusual Biedermeier piece. The case structure is completely veneered in burr birch and ebonized pear, and the mechanism dates circa 1820. The side elevation of the clock is narrow, measuring eight inches in depth, and it rises gracefully off the ground. In addition, it is wider at the base than at the top, a subtly tapered shape characteristic of Berlin designs. In its monumentality, the piece is reminiscent of a pyramid.

The notion of the bourgeois Biedermeier lifestyle was inherent in the production of almost all household objects at the time. What was produced was designed specifically for domestic needs. Just as furniture set the stage for a certain atmosphere within a room, household items carried that notion to its full fruition. A Biedermeier room was definitely the sum of its parts; all was lovingly chosen and placed within the environment to contribute to its full effect.

The Biedermeier household, in the final analysis, was a pastime for the bourgeoisie. Its creation was a full-time process—an expressive and artistic activity—which took shape because of a need for peace, order, and intimacy. In its search for comfort, and the corollary notions of coziness and domesticity, the bourgeoisie sought to forget the wars, the degeneration, and the oppression of earlier times. They created homes in which they could safeguard happiness and love, thereby protecting themselves from conflict. The successful creation of that personal sanctuary was an industrious, creative pursuit, and as such, became the new art form which evolved during the Biedermeier era.

Fig. 180
A Berlin birch and ebonized pear wood grandfather clock with an elegantly tapered pyramid form. PRIVATE COLLECTION, MUNICH

Fig. 181
A south German cherry-veneer and ebonized pear clock. PRIVATE COLLECTION, WEST GERMANY

Chapter 6

Although the term "Biedermeier" aptly describes the furniture, domestic life, and philosophy of the Austrian and German bourgeoisie, it must be applied more selectively to painting. In response to bourgeois patronage, painting and drawing met with popular success in the first half of the nineteenth century. On the whole, paintings in the Biedermeier era sought to hold a mirror to everyday life and reflected the conservative values society placed on such virtues as hard work, diligence, and orderliness. Artists occupied themselves with the narrative of daily life, finding inspiration and subject matter in all aspects of the culture. They portrayed the pristine nature of a preindustrial world with meticulous accuracy and precision.

Paintings served a special function in the Biedermeier home. Since the householder was at ease with the people and surroundings he knew best, he collected a great number of family pictures, views of favorite vacation spots, and local genre scenes, and he hung them in symmetrical arrangements along the walls. These familiar images depicted everyday events in the lives of their owners. As can be seen in renderings of interiors of the period, the pictures were usually small, to suit the modest proportions of the rooms. The Biedermeier artist created an illusion of magnitude by painting his subject at very close range.

Biedermeier landscape painting relied on a realistic technique to express an idealized image of nature. In the meticulous and faithful recording of every detail (real or imagined), an artist could celebrate the charm of a familiar landscape. Biedermeier landscape painting served to bring an idyllic sense of the outdoors inside the walls of the urban bourgeois citizen's home, fulfilling a city dweller's fantasy of being in touch with nature.

Ferdinand Georg Waldmüller (1793–1865) was the quintessential Viennese Biedermeier landscape painter. His landscapes are representations of nature recorded with an almost photographic accuracy. In 1830, Waldmüller was appointed professor of landscape painting at the Viennese Academy, where he was known to stress exact observation of nature as the primary goal of landscape painting.[1] His own views of nature, however, omit any undesirable details, and feature clear blue skies and limpid streams.

Waldmüller's *Maple Trees at Ischl* of 1831 (fig. 184) is a typical Biedermeier landscape. At 31.5 × 26 centimeters (12 × 10 in.), it is a very small painting, but its diminutive size is belied by its

Fig. 182
Still Life of Fruit and Flowers, by Johann Nepomuk Mayrhofer (64 x 50 cm [25⅛ x 19¾ in.]). Signed and dated 1826. Oil on canvas. PRIVATE COLLECTION, NEW YORK CITY

Fig. 183
Portrait of the Artist's Brother and Sister, by Julius Oldach (60 x 90 mm [2½ x 3½ in.]). Pen, ink, and watercolor, circa 1825. PRIVATE COLLECTION, NEW YORK CITY

Fig. 184
Maple Trees at Ischl, by Ferdinand Georg Waldmüller (31.5 x 26 cm [12 x 10 in.]). Oil on canvas. 1831. COLLECTION OF THE VIENNA OSTERREICHISCHE GALERIE

monumental subject matter. The whole image is painted with tiny, meticulous brushstrokes. True to Waldmüller's love of naturalism, every blade of grass and every leaf seems to have been precisely rendered. And there is a touch of typical Biedermeier sentimentality in the image of young children beside a rustic cottage nestled under towering maple trees which, despite their enormous size, seem protective rather than threatening.

Another favorite Biedermeier subject was the interior of a room. Rooms were painted for their own sake, as if they had a good story to tell and the artist had the urge to recount their every delicate detail. Not only were trained artists commissioned to record the particular décor of a room, but family members often attempted more modest depictions of their own in their eagerness to record their personal environment. The character of a room was a highly prized extension of one's life, and, like a familiar friend or relation, the room merited the tribute of having its portrait painted at any opportunity.

In the Biedermeier world, a room reflected a tranquil and harmonious home. Artists conveyed this sense of domestic happiness by painting gentle scenes of quiet activity. One artist who worked in this tradition was the German painter Georg Friedrich Kersting (1785–1847). He specialized in depictions of a single figure, absorbed in concentration, in simple surroundings. Generally, Kersting's figures are viewed from behind, giving the spectator an unself-conscious view of the subject while the peace and privacy of his world is undisturbed. Like the great seventeenth-century Dutch artist Vermeer, Kersting captures bourgeois contentment with sympathy and simplicity. Figures are frequently near a window, where the curtain is pulled back to allow light to enter; a glimpse of the outside world is rarely discernible through the glass.

Kersting's work is repeatedly tinged with Biedermeier sentimentality, and his paintings reflect the characteristic mundane pastimes. In the painting *Young Woman Sewing by Lamplight,* of 1828 (fig. 185), the artist is concerned with the isolation of his subject. The shade is pulled down, but the single lamp on the worktable seems to cast a particularly luminous and warm atmospheric glow. The simple scene of the woman sewing is depicted lovingly and tenderly. Again, the format is small and intimate—the painting measures 38 × 30.5 centimeters (15 × 12 in.). The colors, principally green and shades of brown, ochers and siennas, are natural earth colors. The curtain is rhythmically folded and each dangling tassel on the fringe is carefully painted in, as are the letters on the bookbinding and the webbing of the work basket. The precision of the artist's handling and the privacy of the overall mood are typical Biedermeier characteristics. The artist has portrayed the sitter as

being wholly content in her serene and sparsely furnished environment. Kersting seems to hint that the longings of the human spirit can be comforted by the cozy atmosphere and simple pleasures to be found within four walls.

Because of their intimate nature and small scale, drawings were particularly suited to the Biedermeier room. Family portraits were, of course, sentimental. Often they were done as miniatures, or as silhouettes, underscoring the love of a world of small things. In contrast to eighteenth-century portraiture, in which the sitter was typically shown life-size and was often posed against a nondescript background, Biedermeier portraiture featured its subject in a meticulously documented environment, painstakingly recorded inch by inch.

Children play a significant role in Biedermeier paintings and drawings. There are several possible explanations for this. Certainly, children were a focal point of domestic life and their importance was emphasized in the Biedermeier artist's account of day-to-day existence. But, additionally, perhaps it is important to remember that the middle class had recently survived the devastation of the Napoleonic wars. Those parents who raised children in peacetime must have considered them as a hope for the future; as such, children took on an almost symbolic significance in Biedermeier society —a fact which is reflected by their frequent appearance in paintings of the period.

Figure 186 shows an anonymous portrait of a child in which the artist's attempt to grasp the essence of sweet, innocent childhood is evident. The little girl is seen through the framework of a window (as stated earlier, an important viewpoint in Biedermeier lifestyle and painting, as it stresses the separation of the interior and exterior worlds). The child, who clutches her doll, has had her flouncing curls neatly tucked under a bonnet. The bonnet's undulating brim and wide ribbon are as decorative as the ruffled collar of her dress. Above her, a caged bird (a typical Biedermeier accessory) gazes from his perch. The artist has portrayed his subject tenderly, as if he wants to communicate a sense of joy and security about the child's existence.

Many Viennese artists were important to the development of Biedermeier painting and the interior genre scene. Josef Danhauser (1805–1845), son of the Viennese cabinetmaker, specialized in family groups and interior scenes which often involved children playing. Rudolf von Alt (1812–1905) was another outstanding Austrian Biedermeier artist, remembered principally for his watercolors of European towns and country landscapes, which were very colorful and meticulously executed.

Friedrich von Amerling (1803–1887) was a celebrated Vien-

Fig. 186
Anonymous portrait of a girl at a window. Possibly by Vogel (48 x 43 cm [19 x 17 in.]). Oil on canvas. COLLECTION OF THE DRESDEN STAATLICHE KUNSTSAMMLUNG

Fig. 187
Young Girl with Straw Hat, by Friedrich von Amerling (59 x 47 cm [23 x 18.5 in.]). Oil on canvas. circa 1835. COLLECTION OF NEUE PINAKOTHEK, MUNICH

Fig. 188
Portrait of the Artist's Son with His Dog, by Ferdinand Georg Waldmüller (39.2 x 31.2 cm [15 x 12 in.]). Oil on canvas. 1830. COLLECTION OF NEUE PINAKOTHEK, MUNICH

nese portraitist of the era who specialized in paintings of the bourgeoisie. His work often broke with purely representational realism and achieved a somewhat subjective quality. It is certain that Amerling was influenced by English portraiture, for he studied with Sir Thomas Lawrence in 1827.[2] In his *Young Girl with Straw Hat,* circa 1835 (fig. 187), there is a definite air of bourgeois charm in the sitter's relaxed and pleasing pose. By painting the subject resting her head on her hand, Amerling achieves a charming reflective mood. The close range of the subject and relatively small format of the canvas—59 × 47 centimeters (23 × 18.5 in.)—are typical characteristics of Biedermeier portraiture. The arresting directness of the painting results from both the strong effect of light pouring in from the left and the bravura handling typical of English portrait painting. These are relieved by the soft textures of the girl's clothes and the rich but subtle palette.

Ferdinand Waldmüller, mentioned earlier as a landscape painter, was also a celebrated portraitist. His 1830 *Portrait of the*

194

Artist's Son with his Dog (fig. 188) combines landscape and portraiture, both with an equal concern for realistic detail. Although the virtuous young man in the foreground is the focal point of the painting, the background is rendered with equal care and precise brushstrokes. The vibrant blue of the youth's coat is balanced by forceful greens in the background. Lovingly attentive, his dog completes the idyllic scene. Curiously, the scale of the portrait suggests a certain monumentality, although the canvas size is typically small, measuring 39.2 × 31.2 centimeters (15.5 × 12 in.).

Peter Fendi (1796–1842), another Viennese painter of note during the era, also chose scenes of bourgeois life as subject matter. His painting *Girl in Front of the Lottery Building* (fig. 189) is an anecdotal scene in which the girl's disappointed expression seems to tell the whole story. Such genre scenes, in which an incident from everyday life is focused on and sentimentalized, stem from an eighteenth-century tradition. Fendi's forlorn young lady could be a distant cousin of the heroines of Jean-Baptiste Greuze's genre pictures, with their cracked pitchers, broken eggs, and escaped canaries, though she differs from her eighteenth-century antecedent in that her dilemma speaks for itself, providing a pretext for depicting a pretty face and evoking an empathetic reaction from the viewer—with no moral overtones.

Unlike its Viennese equivalent, German Biedermeier painting existed alongside German Romantic painting. Whereas Biedermeier painting was conservative and full of bourgeois charm, the German Romantic movement, whose central figures were Philipp Otto Runge (1777–1810) and Caspar David Friedrich (1774–1840), was characterized by searching, mystical themes and symbolism. Although both tangents of painting existed side by side, they had very little to do with each other, and to include German romantic painting even briefly in this discussion would not do it justice.

A true Biedermeier painting reflected the prevalent philosophy and character of the bourgeoisie. The common citizen's disposition toward portraits, room interiors, and genre scenes, as well as the conservative nature of the period, ultimately characterize Biedermeier painting as having little to do with German Romanticism. The most successful of the Biedermeier artists found inspiration in nature and all domestic and mundane aspects of their culture. It was with the tangible subject matter of his own environment that the Biedermeier artist reflected back to the viewer the image of a comfortable, happy life lived in a quiet and simple way.

Fig. 189
Girl in Front of the Lottery Building, by Peter Fendi (63 x 50 cm [24.5 x 19.5 in.]). Signed and dated 1829. Oil on canvas. COLLECTION OF THE VIENNA STADTMUSEUM

Conclusion

Under the cloud of the Metternich system, there blossomed with the Biedermeier one of the most charming and sensitive epochs. It is hardly an exaggeration to describe this rich intellectual and artistic development as the consequence and result of a kind of "inward immigration." People . . . withdrew from outward concerns into the intimate circle of the family and friendly relations with their fellow creatures. The harmless, gay parlour game, the sentimental literary salon, the cultivation of music at home: these formed the basis of a widely ramified, deeply rooted cultural life. [1]

As a cultural phenomenon, the Biedermeier period lasted for a generation and then began to change. Between the years 1815 and 1848, Austria and Germany witnessed the transformation from the hand lathe to Thonet's steam press. With the advent of the

Fig. 190
A cherry-veneer and ebonized occasional table with sweeping legs is characteristic of Viennese design. PRIVATE COLLECTION, LOCUST VALLEY, NEW YORK

Fig. 191
An anonymous Biedermeier pencil drawing depicting an afternoon gathering typical of the period. PRIVATE COLLECTION, WEST GERMANY

191

industrial revolution, new technology enhanced the production methods of furniture and eradicated the more obsolete forms of hand craftsmanship. What began as both a skill and an art practiced by individual master craftsmen quickly developed into large-scale industrial production.

The transition from hand-crafted cabinetmaking to early forms of mass production led to a shift in social structure as well. Originally, the Biedermeier family willingly accepted the limitations of censorship and a restrictive society in order to avoid complications with the state. After all, the state, in its paternalistic guise, accepted the responsibility for the citizen's happiness and welfare. But the citizens could not stay insulated, safe from the knowledge of unrest and poverty outside.

The railroad had come to Austria and Germany, and with it news of nationalist movements and Western European liberal ideas. Although the average Biedermeier citizen might not have known it, revolution was in the air and the unification of Germany was only a few years away. The middle class had become commercially and industrially strengthened at the expense of a widening impoverished class. And by the late 1830s, financial conditions in Germany, and all of central Europe, were growing progressively worse. In the midst of the unrest (or perhaps because of the unrest) a German who had been expelled from his own country and from France, Karl Marx, together with Friedrich Engels, published *Das Kommunistische Manifest* (the *Communist Manifesto*). The year was 1848. In his manifesto Marx declared that history was a record of class struggle and that the struggle would end with the creation of a classless society.

No doubt the railroad and the writings of Karl Marx had some effect on ending the Biedermeier era. Metternich's policies had an effect too—they had kept the citizens behind the barriers of censorship and repression for too long. And yet, it was just this attitude, of keeping the problems of the rest of the world at bay and being self-sufficient in art and intellect, that had allowed the Biedermeier period to flourish. Citizens could, and were encouraged to, cultivate and care for the narrow world of their homes. And the Biedermeier artists and craftsmen responded to this focus and profited from it.

The resignation of Metternich, the architect behind the Biedermeier lifestyle, marked the definitive end of an era. After the February 1848 revolutions in Paris, the Viennese began to demonstrate and draw up petitions. At this point Metternich resigned and fled the country, and on March 15 an imperial manifesto abolished censorship and promised that a constitutional assembly would be convened. The peaceful, paternalistic world of Biedermeier had come to a close.

Notions of the pure Biedermeier style had already begun to wane nearly two decades earlier. In the early Biedermeier years, after the Napoleonic wars, the new bourgeoisie in Austria was a malleable society which Metternich and Franz I could easily control; the situation in Germany was similarly managed by heads of state and the "Metternich system." However, the emergence of a new generation of children and new technology by 1830 resulted in a strengthening of the internal structure of the bourgeoisie and the beginnings of new ideals, which replaced the happiness and contentment of being at peace, having children, caring for and embellishing one's home, and becoming financially prosperous.

And, in addition, it is important to remember that many of the creative geniuses associated with the Biedermeier era died during those years of transition. Ludwig van Beethoven and Franz Schubert died in 1827 and 1828, respectively. In 1830 the master craftsman Josef Danhauser, who designed and made more Biedermeier furniture than any other known cabinetmaker, died. In 1832, Johann Wolfgang von Goethe, the great literary genius of his world, died in Weimar, Germany. Austria's ruler, Franz I, whose lifestyle had such an influence on the domestic culture of Biedermeier Vienna, died in 1835. Finally, Berlin's architectural mentor, Karl Friedrich Schinkel, died in 1841.

The end of an era is often symbolized by the death of its cultural leaders. A vacuum appears. New ideas, new tastemakers, and new leaders inevitably replace the old and change the focus and the ideals. And in the second half of the Biedermeier period, there was great innovation concurrent with the absence of creative genius.

And yet, no matter how short-lived Biedermeier culture was, it made its mark on future generations. The functional, unobtrusive, and elegant tenets inherent in Biedermeier design have reoccurred throughout the years. Scandinavian revivals of the period, Biedermeier's influence on turn-of-the-century Vienna, and the current interest in the Biedermeier style are a testament to the fact that good design transcends time and political climate.

Elsie de Wolfe, America's first woman interior decorator, presented Biedermeier to the American public a century after its heyday in Europe. In 1913 she wrote *The House in Good Taste,* in which her ideas on interior decoration were neatly encapsulated in a chapter entitled "Suitability, Simplicity, Proportion." The values reflected by this title mirror the philosophy of early nineteenth-century Biedermeier design. It is no wonder, then, that Elsie de Wolfe used Biedermeier furniture throughout her decorating career, not only by choosing antique pieces, but also by producing contemporary pieces based on Biedermeier design. Compare a lucite chair she

Figs. 195 196
Two examples of Biedermeier
furniture adapted to the
reception area and conference
room of a contemporary office
building. PRIVATE COLLECTION,
WASHINGTON, D.C.

Perhaps the search for a pure, unadorned aesthetic takes its cue in reaction to the lavish and ornamental styles which precede it. In early nineteenth-century Europe, the rich and sumptuous Empire style existed before Biedermeier. At the beginning of the twentieth century, Victorian trappings and ornamental velvets choked a room's light and space. Then came the search for simplicity. In both cases, the notion of simplicity rescued decoration from ornamental abandon. And although the Biedermeier style did become more ornate, Rococo-like, and sumptuous toward the end, it did not suffer from ornamental excess. As a result, almost any Biedermeier piece—with its clean lines and simplified elegance—could fit into a simple contemporary setting today.

It is difficult to assess the current appreciation of the Biedermeier style, since its influence is still spreading. However, we are approaching the end of another century (one parallel), and when all of the curious design mutations of the past decades of this century are considered (just as the decades of the nineteenth century were reappraised at its close), one might ask the following questions: Is it relevant that Biedermeier design, once again, is laying claim to an ever-expanding patronage from decorating, design, architectural, and collecting fields? Are its suitability, simplicity, and proportion (to borrow a phrase) a key to its longevity? Is current machine-made furniture in the Biedermeier style an imitative form of flattery? Finally, will the current enthusiasm fade and reoccur again?

The answer in all cases is probably yes. However, the significant factor is that the Biedermeier style is strengthened as revivals of it fade in and out of fashion. And if the trend is indeed cyclical, we have it to enjoy at the present moment and can take comfort in knowing that it will resurface to inspire future generations.

Fig. 197
Biedermeier furniture is ingeniously incorporated in a modern bathroom—the cherry-veneer mirror is hinged on the wall and opens to reveal a medicine cabinet. Foreground: A Viennese dressing table and chair. PRIVATE COLLECTION, LOCUST VALLEY, NEW YORK

N O T E S

Introduction

1. Georg Himmelheber, *Biedermeier Furniture* (London: Faber & Faber, 1974), p. 53.

2. Ibid., p. 25.

3. Ibid., p. 26.

4. Ibid., p. 28.

5. Kirk Varnedoe, *Vienna 1900: Art, Architecture and Design* (New York: Museum of Modern Art, 1986), p. 85.

1. Domestic Life and the Viennese Interior

1. Charles Osborne, *Schubert and His Vienna* (New York: Alfred A. Knopf, 1985), p. 20.

2. Susan Mary Alsop, *The Congress Dances: Vienna 1814–1815* (New York: Harper & Row, 1984), p. 25.

3. Ibid., p. 106.

4. Osborne, *Schubert and His Vienna*, p. 135.

5. Ibid., p. 134.

6. Marianne Bernhard, *Das Biedermeier* (Düsseldorf: Econ Taschenbuch Verlag, 1983), p. 256.

7. Hermann Glaser, ed., *The German Mind of the 19th Century* (New York: Continuum, 1981), p. 96.

8. Mario Praz, *An Illustrated History of Interior Decoration* (London: Thames & Hudson, 1964), p. 229.

9. Georg Himmelheber, *Biedermeier Furniture* (London: Faber & Faber, 1974), p. 89.

10. Ibid.

2. Biedermeier Design

1. Heidrun Zinnkann, *Mainzer Möbelschreiner der ersten Hälfte des 19. Jahrhunderts* (Frankfurt am Main: Schriften des Historischen Museums Frankfurt am Main, 1985), pp. 146–47.

2. Ibid., p. 144.

3. *Fine English, French and Continental Furniture,* Christie's catalog, November 1986.

4. Georg Himmelheber, *Biedermeier Furniture* (London: Faber & Faber, 1974), p. 65.

5. Witold Rybczynski, *Home: A Short Story of an Idea* (New York: Viking, 1986), p. 97.

6. Himmelheber, *Biedermeier Furniture*, p. 92.

7. Ibid., p. 94.

8. Ibid., p. 91.

9. Ibid., p. 98.

3. Centers of Production

1. George Himmelheber, *Biedermeier Furniture* (London: Faber & Faber, 1974), p. 53.

2. Ibid., p. 54.

3. Ibid., p. 54.

4. Robert Waissenberger, *Vienna in the Biedermeier Era* (New York: Rizzoli, 1986), p. 51.

5. Ibid., p. 145.

6. Himmelheber, *Biedermeier Furniture*, p. 82.

7. Jörn Bahns, *Biedermeier—Möbel Enftchung—Zentren—Typen* (Munich: Keyser, 1979), p. 30.

8. Himmelheber, *Biedermeier Furniture*, p. 65.

9. Ibid., p. 67.

10. Ibid., p. 69.

11. Ibid., p. 70.

4. Furniture Categories

1. Robert Waissenberger, *Vienna in the Biedermeier Era* (New York: Rizzoli, 1986), p. 14.

2. Claus Grimm, *Ausbruch ins Industriezeitalter*, vol. 2 (Munich: Oldenburg, 1985), p. 347.

5. Decorative Objects

1. Gerhart Egger et al., *Vienna in the Age of Schubert* (London: Victoria & Albert Museum, 1979), p. 51.

2. Witold Rybczynski, *Home* (New York: Viking, 1986), p. 141.

3. Egger et al., *Vienna in the Age of Schubert*, p. 65.

4. H. Newman, *An Illustrated Dictionary of Glass* (London: Thames & Hudson, 1977), pp. 200ff.

5. Ibid.

6. Ibid.

7. Ibid.

8. Ibid.

9. Egger et al., *Vienna in the Age of Schubert*, p. 57.

10. Ibid., p. 58.

11. Ibid., p. 59.

12. Ibid., p. 63.

13. Ibid., p. 85.

6. Painting

1. Robert Rosenblum and H. W. Janson, *19th Century Art* (New York: Harry N. Abrams, 1984), p. 172.

Conclusion

1. Charles Osborne, *Schubert and His Vienna* (New York: Alfred A. Knopf, 1985), p. 138.

BIBLIOGRAPHY

Alsop, Susan Mary. *The Congress Dances: Vienna 1814–1815.* Harper & Row, New York, 1984.

Arenhörel, Willmuth. *Eisen Statt Gold Preussischer Eisenkunstguss aus dem Schloss Charlottenburg, dem Berlin Museum und Anderen Sammlungen.* Berlin: Siempelkamp, 1982.

Bahns, Jörn. *Biedermeier—Möbel Entstehung—Zentren—Typen.* Munich: Keyser, 1979.

Berlin National Gallery, Orangerie of Schloss Charlottenburg. *Karl Friedrich Schinkel: Architektur, Malerei, Kunstgewerbe.* Berlin: Verwaltung der Staatlichen Schlösser und Gärten Schloss Charlottenburg, 1981.

Bernhard, Marianne. *Das Biedermeier.* Düsseldorf: Econ Taschenbuch Verlag, 1983.

Boch, Helmut, and Wolfgang Heise, eds. *Unzeit des Biedermeiers: Historische Miniaturen zum Deutschen Vormärz 1830 bis 1848.* Cologne: Pahl-Rugenstein, 1986.

Böhmer, Gunter. *Die Welt des Biedermeier.* Munich: Verlagsgesellschaft, 1968.

Buchsbaum, Maria. *Ferdinand Georg Waldmüller.* Salzburg: Residenz Verlag, 1976.

Darby, Michael. "The Viennese at Home, Biedermeier Interiors." *Country Life* (January 25, 1979): 204–7.

De Groër, Leon. *Decorative Arts in Europe 1790–1850.* New York: Rizzoli, 1986.

Dewiel, Lydia. *Biedermeier.* Munich: Wilhelm Heyne Verlag, 1977.

Dorian, Donna. "The Biedermeier Factor: How Michael Graves Has Adopted, and Adapted, a Nineteenth Century Style." *Art & Antiques* (September 1986): 61–62.

Eberlein, H. Donaldson, and Abbot McClure. "The Biedermeier Style: Its Place in Furniture Design and Decoration." *Good Furniture* (July 1916): 29–39.

Egger, Hanna. *Herrn Biedermeiers Wunschbillet.* Vienna: Austrian Museum of Applied Arts, 1978.

Faber, Annette. "Ein Berliner Sekretär des Frühen Biedermeier: Kind des Revolutionären Klassizismus." *Kunst & Antiquitäten* IV (1985): 62–66.

Finke, Ulrich. *German Painting from Romanticism to Expressionism.* London: Thames and Hudson, 1974.

Geismeier, Willi. *Biedermeier Kunst und Kultur.* Leipzig: VEB E. A. Seemann Verlag, 1979.

————. *Malerei des Biedermeier.* Leipzig: VEB E. A. Seemann Verlag, 1981.

Glaser, Hermann, ed. *The German Mind of the 19th Century: A Literary and Historical Anthology.* New York:

Continuum, 1981.

Grimm, Claus. *Ausbruch ins Industriezeitalter.* Munich: Oldenburg, 1985.

Hederer, Oswald. *Leo von Klenze.* Munich: Verlag Georg D. W. Callwey, 1964.

Hellich, Erika. *Alt-Wiener Uhren Die Sammlung Sobek im Geyermüller-Schlössl 1750–1900.* Munich: Verlag Georg D. W. Callwey, and Vienna: Austrian Museum of Applied Arts, 1978.

Himmelheber, Georg. "Biedermeier." *Connoisseur* (May 1979): 2–15.

———. *Biedermeier Furniture.* S. Jervis, trans. London: Faber & Faber, 1974.

———. "Des Preussen Konigs Krankenstuhl." *Die Weltkunst* 9 (May 5, 1986): 1286.

Kleeblatt, Norman, and Vivian Mann. *Treasures of the Jewish Museum.* New York: Universe Books, 1986.

Koch, Horst. *Wiener Biedermeier.* Kirchdorf-Inn, West Germany: Berghaus Verlag, 1977.

Kovachek, Michael. *Glas aus vier Jahrhunderten.* Vienna: Glasgalerie Michael Kovachek, 1982.

Kreisel, Heinrich, and Georg Himmelheber. *Die Kunst des Deutschen Möbels, Klassizismus Historismus, Jugendstil.* Munich: C. H. Beck Verlag, 1973.

Krüger, Renate. *Biedermeier Eine Lebenshaltung Zwischen 1815 und 1848.* Vienna: Edition Tusch, 1979.

Leitich, Ann Tizia. *Wiener Biedermeier, Kultur, Kunst und Leben der Alten Kaiserstadt vom Wiener Kongress bis zum Stumjahr 1848.* Leipzig: Bielefeld, 1941.

Lux, Joseph August. *Von der Empirezur Biedermeierzeit: eine Sammlung characteristicher Möbel und Innenräume.* Stuttgart, 1906.

Mundt, Barbara. *Berliner Eisen-der Preussische Eisenkunstguss des 19 Jahrhunderts.* Berlin: Staatliche Museen Preussischer Kulturbesitz, 1986.

Nagel, Fritz. *Möbel.* Munich: Battenberg Verlag, 1977.

Neuwith, Waltraud. *Biedermeiertassen Formen und Dekore am Biespiel des Wiener Porzellans.* Munich: Schneider-Henn, 1982.

Osborne, Charles. *Schubert and His Vienna.* New York: Alfred A. Knopf, 1985.

Pazaurek, Gustav, and Eugen Philippovich. *Gläser der Empire und Biedermeierzeit.* Braunschweig: Klinkhardt & Biermann, 1976.

Praz, Mario. *An Illustrated History of Interior Decoration.* London: Thames and Hudson, 1964.

Pressler, Rudolf, and Robin Straub. *Biedermeier-Möbel.* Munich: Battenberg Verlag, 1986.

Rybczynski, Witold. *Home: A Short Story of an Idea.* New York: Viking, 1986.

Spiegel, Walter. *Dekorative Graphik Barock bis Biedermeier.* Munich: Wilhelm Heyne Verlag, 1980.

Stamm, Brigette. *Blick auf Berliner Eisen.* Berlin: Verwaltung der Staatlichen Schlösser und Gärten, 1979.

Thornton, Peter. *Authentic Decor: The Domestic Interior 1620–*

1920. New York: Viking, 1984.

Varnedoe, Kirk. *Vienna 1900: Art, Architecture and Design.* New York: Museum of Modern Art, 1986.

Vaughan, William. *German Romantic Painting.* New Haven: Yale University Press, 1980.

Vetter, Robert. "Herr Biedermeier in Vienna." *Antiques* (December 1983): 698–705.

Vienna in the Age of Schubert: The Biedermeier Interior 1815–1848. London: Victoria and Albert Museum, 1979. Catalog.

Von Boehn, Max. *Biedermeier, Deutschland von 1815–1847.* Berlin, n.d.

Von Herzogenberg, Johanna. *Mähren: Malerische Ansichten aus Romantik und Biedermeier.*

Munich: Adalbert Foundation, and Vienna: Austrian Museum of Applied Arts, 1975.

Waissenberger, Robert, ed. *Vienna in the Biedermeier Era.* New York: Rizzoli, 1986.

Windisch-Graetz. "Le Bon Goût Selon Monsieur Biedermeier." *Connaissance des Arts* 91 (1959): 76–83.

Wirth, Irmgard. *Bürgerliches Leben im Berliner Biedermeier.* Berlin: Berlin Museum, 1978.

Witt-Dörring, Christian. "Wiener Möbeleschläge 1810–1834." *Die Weltkunst* 21 (1985): 3197–99.

Zinnkann, Heidrun. *Mainzner Mobelsschreiner der ersten Hälfte des 19 Jahrhunderts.* Frankfurt am Main: Historisches Museum Frankfurt am Main, 1985.

Index